Original title:
Blossoms of the Bard

Copyright © 2025 Creative Arts Management OÜ
All rights reserved.

Author: Charles Whitfield
ISBN HARDBACK: 978-1-80567-075-9
ISBN PAPERBACK: 978-1-80567-155-8

The Tapestry of the Blooming Mind

In a garden where thoughts take flight,
Ideas sprout like flowers at night.
They dance with glee, a comical sight,
Tickling petals, oh what sheer delight!

A jester juggles thoughts on a swing,
While daisies giggle, their joy they bring.
Laughter erupts, like a springtime fling,
As the sun winks, and the robins sing.

Old weeds of doubt try to crash the show,
But the daisies insist, 'Come join the flow!'
With clay pots and dreams, we paint it so,
In this funny garden, we let our minds grow.

So gather, dear friends, with a wink and a grin,
Let's sprinkle some laughter, and let the fun begin.
In this quirky realm, where ideas spin,
With a tug at your heart, and a tickle within.

Quietude Among the Blooms

In a garden, bees are snore,
Telling tales of floral lore.
Petals fall, the bees just yawn,
Finding snooze from dusk till dawn.

Frogs croak jokes, the crickets laugh,
Chasing moths, a wild baffle path.
Sunlight winks with playful glee,
Nature's nap, as calm as can be.

Resonance of the Earth's Heart

The flowers sing in silly tunes,
Dancing 'neath the laughing moons.
A dandelion wears a hat,
While squirrels plot a joke or chat.

Worms perform a wiggly show,
Telling secrets no one knows.
Grasshoppers leap with perfect flair,
Dreaming up a wacky air.

Sowing Seeds of Expression

Planting seeds of silly thought,
In this soil, fun is sought.
The veggies giggle, shout hooray,
As gobbles come from birds at play.

Sunflowers strut in the breeze,
Waving hello with leafy fees.
Laughter grows where roots align,
Each sprout joined in comic line.

The Landscape of Emotion

A hill made of chuckles and cheer,
With clouds that twirl, bringing near.
Each breeze whispers a playful tease,
Making hearts hum with sweet ease.

Rivers giggle while they flow,
Making puddles where laughter grows.
Joking trees sway to a tune,
Crash of humor beneath the moon.

Raindrops on Velvet Petals

Raindrops dance on silky blooms,
Tickling leaves with playful grooms.
A splash here, a splash there,
Who knew flowers had such flair?

Bees wear tiny raincoats too,
Buzzing tunes like they're in a zoo.
A flower sneezes, pollen flies,
And all the critters laugh and sigh.

The Poetry of Blooming Time

Daisies recite in the afternoon,
About the grasshopper's wild tune.
Each petal's a verse, soft and sweet,
Poems emerge in the garden's heat.

Lilies giggle when the wind blows,
Whispering secrets only they know.
A daffodil cracks a joke in rhyme,
While tulips tap dance in their prime.

Stanzas in the Sunlight

Sunshine paints the flowers' glow,
Tickled toes with a bright yellow show.
The violets burst into fits of joy,
Swaying like they've found a new toy.

Petunias play hide and seek all day,
"Your turn to bloom!" they laugh and sway.
Butterflies join in, swirling around,
A comic ballet on the ground.

Wreaths of Words and Nature

Wreaths of petals, words that twirl,
A garland smile, a flower girl.
Each leaf waving, saying, "Steal a glance!"
Nature's verses in a merry dance.

The roses crack jokes with the thyme,
"Thyme flies when you're having a rhyme!"
In the garden, laughter fills the air,
With every bloom, a moment to share.

Garden of the Quill

In a garden where words grow,
The quill dances to and fro.
Puns bloom bright like daffodils,
Each scribble cheered with silly thrills.

A squirrel steals a rhyming verse,
While poets giggle, for better or worse.
The sunflowers nod to the punchlines made,
As honeybees sip from the jokes we laid.

Whispers of the Muse

A muse with a wink, so sly and spry,
Whispers secrets to passersby.
Her laughter spills like bubbles in air,
Tickling the ears of those who dare.

With sonnets that slip on banana peels,
And limericks wrapped in surreal feels,
The ink stains those who ponder too long,
Their thoughts now dance to a comical song.

A Tapestry of Stanzas

Threads of humor weave through the lines,
In this quirky tapestry, laughter shines.
Each stanza a patch of mischief and glee,
Where giggles and grins roam wild and free.

A cat in a top hat, a dog on a bike,
In the fabric of wit, they share a strike.
With twirls and loops, the pages unfold,
Tales stitched with chuckles, a sight to behold.

The Fragrance of Rhyme

Rhyme wafts through the garden in style,
Mixing up puns with a fragrant smile.
A bouquet of words, all silly and bright,
Each petal a punchline that takes off in flight.

The daisies chuckle, the roses burst out,
As poets parade with a whimsical shout.
A sonnet in perfume, making you grin,
In this fragrant realm, let the fun begin.

Petals of Prose

In a garden where words are sprout,
A pun took root, have no doubt.
With every phrase, the giggles grow,
As laughter dances in a row.

Syntax winks beneath the sun,
Each metaphor a playful pun.
As petals tickle noses bright,
The humor blooms, a pure delight.

The verbs just can't keep still, you see,
They jiggle with glee, so wild and free.
Nouns trip over, fall in heaps,
Creating joy that never sleeps.

So come and join this merry spree,
Where every line's a chuckling spree.
Among these fun-filled stanzas find,
Delightful quirks, the frolic of mind.

Verses in Bloom

In the garden of silly rhymes,
The daisies dance to silly chimes.
Each couplet jests, the buds reply,
With giggles bursting from the sky.

A joke's a seed, it's quick to grow,
Sprouting laughter, row by row.
In every line, the chuckles blend,
As humor's fragrance has no end.

The sonnets sway, with teasing grace,
Each quatrain wears a goofy face.
They whisper secrets to the breeze,
While punsters giggle 'neath the trees.

So gather 'round this playful plot,
Where smiles bloom like flowers hot.
In every verse, find joy and cheer,
As this bouquet of jest draws near.

The Flowers of Lyricism

In verses where the giggle grows,
The lilies wear their finest clothes.
With petals bright, they sing aloud,
    Enticing every jester crowd.

Rhymes mingle like a funny stew,
    Potatoes laugh, and carrots too.
Chorus of chuckles, soft and sweet,
    In this garden, we're all elite.

Every stanza's a waltz, a jig,
With rhythmic roots that dance so big.
The blooms of humor stretch and twist,
In playful verses that can't be missed.

So grab a friend and join the cheer,
Where laughter's fragrance fills the sphere.
In this field of witty charms,
    Every flower sings, no alarms!

Echoes of the Spring Sonnet

In springtime's breath, the jokes take flight,
With rollicking words that feel just right.
Hares and turtles race in fun,
Each line a treat, a witty pun.

The daffodils boast heights and dreams,
While tulips plot their funny schemes.
Each petal holds a comic tale,
As laughter dances on the trail.

The haikus giggle with bright flair,
Sprinkling smiles in the spring air.
Each verse a bloom, delightfully light,
Crafting sunshine from day to night.

So wander through this playful glade,
Where mirth and magic interlade.
In every echo, let joy be found,
In this garden, fun knows no bound.

Nature's Ballad in Color

In the garden, flowers dance,
With bees in bloom, they take a chance.
Petals wear a sunlit grin,
While worms below are doing spin.

Colors clash, a patchwork bright,
Lilies laugh at morning light.
Tulips gossip with a breeze,
As daisies tease with playful ease.

Butterflies in silly flight,
Flaunt their shades, a pure delight.
Bumblebees with buzzing song,
Join the fun where they belong.

Nature's jesters, bold and free,
In this realm of harmony.
They twirl and spin till the day's end,
In joyful chaos, they descend.

The Lyrical Meadow

In the meadow, laughter swells,
With dandelions ringing bells.
A rabbit hops with silly grace,
While crickets cheer the funny race.

Each flower wears a fuzzy hat,
As painters dip in shades of chat.
Sunflowers prance, they think they're stars,
While clovers hum in nearby bars.

A breeze tickles the grass so high,
As butterflies begin to fly.
With every flap, a giggle burst,
In this meadow, joy's rehearsed.

So dance around, ye green and grand,
Join the whimsy, take a stand.
For laughter blooms in every hue,
In nature's heart, a playful crew.

Enchanted Petals of Prose

In the forest, words take flight,
Roses whisper, wild with spite.
Tulips frown in clever jest,
With petals soft, they're quite the best.

A pinecone stumbled on a rhyme,
Fell on a pun, oh such a crime.
The willow weeps, but not in pain,
Just finds it funny, shades of gain.

Though squirrels plot, a nutty crew,
Their jokes take root in laughter's dew.
Bamboo giggles, swaying slow,
With every sway, a tale to show.

So come and hear the trees recite,
Their stories deep and full of light.
Each petal spun from laughter's loom,
In every blink, a joyful bloom.

The Garden's Gentle Muse

In the garden, mischief brews,
With butterflies and laughing hues.
Zinnias wear a crooked smile,
As roses tease and chat awhile.

Beans that climb and twist in glee,
They form a band, just wait and see.
Radishes play hide and seek,
While veggies plot, their jokes unique.

Cucumbers with their pickle wit,
They roll with laughter, never quit.
And sunflowers, tall, they reign supreme,
In this garden, all has a theme.

So grab a seat upon the grass,
Join in the fun, just let it pass.
For in this patch, oh what a muse,
Laughter and joy, you cannot lose.

Vibrant Verses in the Air

In a garden where jokes grow,
Laughter comes and starts to flow.
Dancing leaves and silly bees,
Whisper rhymes in every breeze.

Petals giggle, colors tease,
Swaying gently with such ease.
Every line a playful jest,
Wordplay wears its very best.

Here the sun wears glasses bright,
Moonbeams dance in pure delight.
Daffodils are plotting schemes,
Tickling everyone with dreams.

Join the fun, don't be a bore,
Come and laugh forevermore.
In this joy-filled, joyful place,
Words and giggles interlace.

Spheres of Imagination

Imagined worlds come alive,
Where silly thoughts take a dive.
Balloon animals float about,
Making everyone laugh out loud.

Clouds wear hats, umbrellas dance,
Every dream gets a chance.
Squirrels sing with funny flair,
Whirling 'round without a care.

Creativity takes a swing,
Ideas sprout like butterflies' wings.
A paintbrush tickles the sky,
Colors laugh, and so do I!

Join this circus in your mind,
Let your dreams be unconfined.
In this realm of whimsy bright,
Everything feels just right.

The Blossom's Ode

A bud broke free with a cackle,
Tickling petals, causing a crackle.
They stretch and giggle in the sun,
This bloom knows how to have fun.

With each sunbeam, laughter swells,
Stories sing from flowery shells.
In a garden full of quips,
Sugar sprinkles on their lips.

Thorns wear crowns of silly hats,
Fluttering past like happy bats.
Every flower has a tale,
Of dancing ants and windy gales.

So lift your spirits, let them soar,
Join the humor evermore.
In this vivid, joyous glow,
Giggles sprout and never slow.

Colors of the Written Word

Each word is like a splash of paint,
Some are rosy, some are quaint.
Scribbles dance on every page,
Jokes unfold with every stage.

Blue ink giggles in a line,
While red whispers, "Isn't this fine?"
Green words bounce in playful glee,
Saying, "Oh, just read with me!"

The paper flutters, starts to sway,
As sentences come out to play.
Adjectives wear polka dots,
While nouns come dressed in silly spots.

So grab a pen and make a mess,
Join this colorful, fun confess.
In each letter, laughter swirls,
As the written word unfurls.

A Symphony of Petal and Page

A page turned, the petals twirl,
Ink spills, as laughter curls.
A sonnet sings to bees in flight,
While daisies chuckle, hearts feel light.

A leaf drops down with a silly sound,
The trees all giggle, joy unbound.
Squirrels dance in a poet's rhyme,
Nature's humor, a jolly mime.

So toss your quill, let the ink run wild,
In this garden, we're all beguiled.
With every line, a chuckle soon,
As petals prance beneath the moon.

Laughter rings in every writing nook,
Where every flower is a playful book.
So raise your pen, let giggles soar,
In this symphony, we all want more!

The Roots of Inspiration

In the soil, the ideas sprout,
Strange thoughts dance, without a doubt.
A carrot sings while potatoes croon,
While turnips wiggle beneath the moon.

The funny roots joke and share,
About their dreams and leafy hair.
They plot and scheme beneath the ground,
Happy whispers, a joyful sound.

Fruits of laughter bloom with glee,
As vegetables recite poetry.
Each sprout a poet, unique and bright,
Writing verses till the fall of night.

So dig the earth, let humor grow,
Create a garden of laughter's flow.
With every seed, a jest will sprout,
In the world of roots, there's no doubt!

Lyrical Petal Dance

In the breeze, the flowers sway,
Tickling petals in a playful way.
Each bloom laughs in bright array,
As dandelions steal the day.

A rose whispers to the daisies near,
"Can you hear the songs? They're crystal clear!"
With pollen as the stage, they prance,
Every blossom joins the dance.

Butterflies waltz with a fluttering tease,
Grasshoppers hop with ridiculous ease.
Frogs join in with ribbits loud,
Their rhythmic croaks forming a crowd.

So sway with joy, let laughter reign,
In this lyrical petal domain.
With every dance, a smile to share,
Nature's humor fills the air!

Fables Flowering

Once upon a sprout of green,
A dandelion gave a grin obscene.
"Why chase the sun, oh daffodil?"
"I thrive in shadows, what a thrill!"

A lavender shared tales of woe,
Of snooty roses, all aglow.
"But I'm just fine," she said with glee,
"'Cause bees prefer my humble plea."

The daisies plotted, in a huddle tight,
"Let's prank the gardener late tonight!"
They dug in dirt while giggling loud,
Yet they still bloomed, and felt so proud.

So raise a glass to flowers bright,
With fables flowering in pure delight.
Each petal holds a story true,
Of laughs and schemes, and bloopers too!

Narrative Nectar

In the garden where words are spun,
A butterfly thinks it's a ton of fun.
It flutters and flaps with a comedic flair,
While bees gawk and mumble, 'Is that thing rare?'

A rhyme out of place, quite a sight to behold,
The sunflowers giggle, their yellow hearts bold.
They sway to the tune of a wordy parade,
While crickets croak out a serenade.

A poet arrives with a quill and some ink,
And misunderstands what the sunflowers think.
They blush, they chuckle, with petals like cheer,
As they try to avoid all that quick-scribbling fear.

In this garden of jest where the verses do play,
Each line is a joke, each stanza a ray.
So join in the laughter, let the humor unfurl,
For poetry's nectar is a riotous whirl.

Enchanted Garden of Words

In a patch of green where the oddball blooms,
The daisies told jokes about comfort and rooms.
A rose blushed so red at the punchline it heard,
While a daffodil snorted, quite absurd.

The weeds joined in, trying to get a laugh,
But their humor was dry, like a math teacher's staff.
Yet, the lily laughed on, with a giggle and sway,
Saying, 'Life's like a garden; it grows in its way!'

A toad sat down, with a grin on his face,
"Why did the flower cross over the space?
To prove he wasn't a chicken, that's why!"
The marigolds chuckled, "Oh me, oh my!"

This whimsical patch holds magic and jest,
Where puns bloom like petals, forever impressed.
So grab a bouquet of laughter and word,
In the land of the clever, let joy be inferred.

The Poet's Bloom

In a meadow where thoughts hilariously grow,
A poet sat pondering what's funny, oh no!
He tripped on a line that was tangled in grass,
And chuckled at rhymes that all seemed to pass.

His verses did waltz like a fawn on a spree,
While squirrels giggled, "Is that poetry?"
A line about muffins, then banana peels,
Had the daisies all rolling, with squeals and with squeals!

Each quip was a bloom, in this light-hearted ball,
The sky turned to canvas and laughter stood tall.
With humor as nectar, he penned without care,
And the wildflowers danced, in their whimsical air.

So let's raise a toast to the poet's delight,
With each giggling flower that blossoms in sight.
For in this odd patch where the silly takes flight,
Lies the truth of the heart; we find joy in the light.

Wildflower Verses

Among scattered petals, there's chaos and cheer,
The wildflowers giggle, they just want a beer!
With puns in their stems, the dandelions say,
"Life's too short, let's bloom while we play!"

A bumblebee buzzed, with a quirk in his flight,
"Why do flowers sing under starlight so bright?
Because they can't find a place to unwind,
So they hum on their leaves, feeling heavenly aligned!"

The violets chimed in, adorned with their crown,
"How about a festival, let's paint the town brown!"
Their voices like petals, scattered through air,
In a floral conundrum, oh what a rare affair!

So gather the laughter, let joy be your guide,
In this garden of whims, where we all take a ride.
With verses of wildflowers, let humor ignite,
As we dance through the petals, free spirits in flight.

Sprouts of Imagination

In a garden where ideas sprout,
Laughter echoes, there's no doubt.
A talking tree tells jokes so sly,
While bees in bow ties buzz on by.

Dancing gnomes on mushrooms twirl,
Singing songs that whirl and whirl.
The flowers giggle, shaking heads,
As rabbits play on colorful beds.

Each petal wears a silly hat,
With socks mismatched, how about that?
A squirrel juggles acorns galore,
In a world where fun's never a bore.

So come and join this grand parade,
Where imagination's always played.
With every bloom, a jest is spun,
In this garden, life's just pure fun!

The Bard's Hidden Grove

In the grove where whispers dwell,
The old oak sings, and all is well.
With fruit that glows like disco lights,
The critters host the wackiest sights.

A raccoon dons a cloak so grand,
Reciting verse on mischief planned.
While hedgehogs juggle thorny dreams,
As the sun spills golden beams.

Chirping frogs play lutes so sweet,
While turtles compete in a silly feat.
The flowers sway to the rhythm's beat,
Creating harmony, oh so neat!

So tiptoe softly, take a peep,
Into this grove where giggles seep.
A world of whimsy, fun, and cheer,
For all who wander, come and leer!

The Canopy of Creativity

Beneath the branches, ideas bloom,
Crafted with laughter, banishing gloom.
The chattering leaves tell witty tales,
Of pirate ships and wind-fueled sails.

A parrot squawks a joke or two,
While squirrels sketch dreams that feel brand new.
Canvas skies filled with color bright,
As owls plan parties deep in the night.

Clouds shape-shift to silly forms,
Dancing through the playful storms.
With every horn blown, laughter swirls,
In the canopy where magic twirls.

So grab a brush, and paint the air,
With joy and jest beyond compare.
Let creativity's spark ignite,
In a leafy world so light and bright!

Petals Folding into Verse

Petals fold with a cheeky grin,
Whispering secrets where rhymes begin.
The daisies argue over the best,
While butterflies compete for a jest.

A bumblebee sings off-key, oh my!
Spinning stories that make you cry.
A sunflower tries to pull a prank,
But tumbles down, and oh, how they sank!

The tulips join in with a cheer,
Creating rhymes we all hold dear.
As ladybugs dance in a grand ballet,
Turning the garden into a play.

So gather round, let's weave this fun,
With petals and puns under the sun.
In every fold and every line,
The joy of verse is simply divine!

The Chorus of Blossoming Life

In a garden where giggles grow,
Flowers dance in a sunlit show.
Bees wear hats and skip about,
While worms play drums with a wiggly shout.

Tulips tease with colors bright,
Swaying gaily, what a sight!
Even roses laugh and sing,
Feeling like the spring's own king.

Daisies tell jokes, oh so sly,
While ladybugs roll by and sigh.
With every breeze, joy takes flight,
In this garden of pure delight!

So join the fun, don't delay,
Let laughter bloom and joyous play.
For in this patch where smiles thrive,
Life's silly side surely comes alive!

Hidden Verses of the Garden

In the corner, a shy bloom hides,
Whispering secrets where humor abides.
The daisies gossip, oh so grand,
About the antics of the nearby land.

Bees are buzzed about the snacks,
Pollinating with their little acts.
Yet ants march in their tiny lines,
Creating chaos in search of vines.

Oh, what fun the petals weave,
Crafting tales that we believe.
A cucumber wears a leafy hat,
Proclaiming, "I am a sprightly chat!"

So listen close, and keep your ears,
Open to laughter among the spheres.
For hidden verses bloom and play,
In this garden, let joy stay!

The Silence of Petal Dreams

In the stillness of the night,
Petal dreams take sudden flight.
They chuckle softly, share some puns,
Underneath the moonlit runs.

A daffodil dreams of wacky shoes,
While the violets choose silly hues.
A sleeping bee with a tiny snore,
Makes petals giggle, wanting more!

In moonlit laughter, they all unite,
Painting dreams in pure delight.
With every twinkling star above,
They spread their magic, fun, and love.

So while the world in slumber waits,
Petal dreams unlock the gates.
To a realm where joy and jests,
Allow our hearts to feel their best!

Colors Caught in Quatrains

A palette spills in hues so bright,
Painting flowers with sheer delight.
Red tulips flatter, yellow roses tease,
In this colorful garden, we're sure to please.

The violets giggle in their blue attire,
While sunflowers bask in morning fire.
Each color whispers a playful rhyme,
Creating joy, transcending time.

Petals dance in a vibrant swirl,
As butterflies spin, giving twirls.
A sunflower grins with golden rays,
Telling tales of silly days.

Oh, the colors in this grand display,
Catch our hearts and lead the way.
To a garden where laughter flows,
In quatrains bright, the fun just grows!

Petals of Reflection

In the garden where jokes take flight,
Petals giggle under the light.
Bees wear hats, buzzing out a tune,
While daisies dance with a playful swoon.

Worms in glasses read the grass,
Cracking puns as the sun does pass.
A squirrel juggles acorns with glee,
Who knew plants held such a comedy spree?

Laughter ripples through leaves so green,
Petals whisper tales, oh what a scene!
Nature's stage where the oddball shines,
In a world where humor intertwines.

So come sit beneath the laughing tree,
Join in the fun, it's a sight to see!
For in this garden, laughter will bloom,
Turning every frown into joyous room.

The Rhyme in Every Bud

In the dew-kissed morn, a sentiment stirs,
Each bud's a poet, spinning sweet purrs.
They write their lines in fragrant air,
With petals soft, they never despair.

Tulips trumpet jokes that just can't wait,
While roses blush at the silliest fate.
Lilies play hopscotch, hopping on air,
Their laughter mingles without a care.

Hyacinths murmur rhymes, oh so slick,
As bees play tag—nature's comedy trick.
Every bud holds a line worth a chuckle,
In this whimsical symphony, hearts will snuggle.

So heed the wisdom of petals in play,
Life's nonsense can brighten up your day!
For in the garden, the rhymes never cease,
Each giggle blossoms, bringing sweet peace.

Enigmas of the Greenery

Amongst the leaves, some secrets lie,
Plants gear up for a cheerful hi-fi.
The ferns whisper riddle, the ivy does sway,
With laughter encoded in shades of the day.

A cactus sings of pricks and pokes,
While lilies tease with botanical jokes.
Who knew greenery had such wit?
Responding with humor, bit by bit.

The hedges snicker, mixing it up,
With every sprout serving a quirky cup.
While thyme and basil plot their play,
Knowing all puns will come back their way.

In the heart of this leafy recess,
Nature's enigmas bring joy, no less.
So meander through, don't hesitate,
For the greenest laughter is simply first-rate.

Garden of Whispered Verse

In a plot where humor hides in the shade,
Plants script comedies, unafraid.
With giggles sprouting near every vine,
The garden's a stage where worries decline.

The sunflowers chuckle with faces so bright,
As pansies gossip from morning to night.
Chives take jabs, and ferns jump around,
In this arena, pure laughter is found.

Sweet peas tell tales of their silly fights,
While roses subsist on comedic delights.
Every bloom has a punchline to share,
Crafting a world that's stripped of despair.

So wander through this patch of delight,
Where flowers and folly take glorious flight.
Each whispered verse, a giggle's embrace,
In this garden, humor finds its place.

The Hidden Sonnet of the Woods

Amid the trees, a squirrel sings,
Chasing dreams with acorn rings.
The owl hoots jokes, a twisty plot,
While mushrooms dance, a giddy lot.

A wily fox in shades of red,
Wears leafy hats atop his head.
The brook joins in, a giggling flow,
Tickling stones with a playful glow.

Woodpeckers tap a rhythmic beat,
While rabbits hop on nimble feet.
In laughter's shade, the shadows play,
A leafy scene where pranks hold sway.

So wander here, where fun is free,
In nature's heart, a comedy.
The forest whispers, wild and bold,
Its secret tales will soon unfold.

Whimsies in the Wildflowers

In petals bright, the daisies wink,
While bees in bow ties sip their drink.
The butterflies wear polka dots,
And gossip blooms in colorful spots.

A ladybug with tiny shoes,
Struts through grass with nothing to lose.
The tulips giggle, dip, and sway,
As daisies boast of yesterday.

In this field, hilarity thrives,
Where nature laughs and joy connives.
Pick a flower, make a wish,
And join the fun with every swish!

So twirl in petals, laugh, and spin,
In whimsical fields, let joy begin.
The flowers hum a merry song,
Join their dance, you can't go wrong!

Flows of Fragrant Prose

In gardens rich, the scents collide,
With onions charming, side by side.
The rosemary tells tales so sweet,
While thyme pranks by the garlic's feet.

A basil leaf, with laughter loud,
Shares secrets of the cheering crowd.
The carrots chuckle underground,
While peas pop up, all round and sound.

Each herb a character, bold and bright,
With witty banter, pure delight.
In fragrant prose, the veggies play,
A comedy on display today.

So savor scents that tickle the nose,
In this garden where humor grows.
Join the feast, don't be late,
For laughter's spice is truly great!

Serenity in the Shade

Under leaves where sunbeams hide,
A sleepy cat takes life in stride.
With yawns that stretch from here to there,
She dreams of fish and fluffy air.

Beside her, ants march with great zeal,
Forming lines, that's quite the deal!
A lazy dog joins in the fun,
Chasing shadows from the sun.

The breeze whispers jokes to the trees,
As squirrels plot their nut-filled pleas.
A chipmunk grins, its cheeks like puffs,
In this shade, the laughter's rough.

So linger here, where time can bend,
In nature's arms, let joy extend.
For in the shade, with giggles near,
Serenity blooms; it's crystal clear.

Growing Lines

In a garden where the sentences sprout,
Words dance around, spinning in and out.
Like daisies that giggle when tickled by sun,
Each rhyme is a prank, a linguistic pun.

With each playful twist, the phrases unwind,
Puns and jokes blossom, uniquely designed.
The laughter of verses, it never does tire,
They tickle the air like a sweet, funny fire.

Each line finds a partner, a rhythmful sway,
A waltz made of giggles, in playful display.
Like weeds of the mind, they grow with delight,
In the maze of imagination, they frolic and fight.

So gather your words and let laughter flow,
In the garden of lines, let the fun overflow.
For every sweet stanza that blooms on the page,
Is a lighthearted jest that deserves a grand stage.

The Hidden Orchard of Thought

In the corners of thought, where the laughter resides,
There's an orchard of chaos that joyfully hides.
With fruit made of puns and the sweetest of spins,
Each thought is a giggle that bubbles and grins.

Tangled branches of ideas, a whimsical maze,
Where logic takes breaks and whimsical plays.
The apples are rhymes, ripe for the picking,
And the oranges of wisdom, they're always quick-witting.

Be wary, dear friend, of the bananas that slip,
For with every bright peal, you may lose your grip.
But laughter is worth every comical fall,
In the hidden orchard, we'll gather it all.

So come take a stroll through this jolly delight,
Where thoughts turn to giggles, and days fill with light.
For life's much too serious without a good jest,
In this secret retreat, we find all that's best.

Ink-Stained Petals

With a quill dipped in laughter, I scribble and scrawl,
The ink-stained petals are ready to sprawl.
Each petal a punchline, fragrant with cheer,
In the garden of giggles, we're never severe.

From the stem of a sentence, a joke takes its flight,
Twisting and twirling, a pure sheer delight.
They brush past the sunbeams, each word taking wing,
As the buzzing of laughter makes all our hearts sing.

Scribbles turn to blooms in the vibrant spring air,
Playful phrases take rest on the branches laid bare.
With petals of humor, they flutter and fold,
In this wild little world, we find treasures of gold.

So join in the fun of this ink-blotted spree,
Where every word sprouted is silly and free.
In the garden of verses, let your laughter swell,
With ink-stained petals, we flourish so well.

Harmonies of the Heart

In a choir of chuckles, the heart sings so loud,
Melodies muddle and joyfully crowd.
With harmonies silly and rhythms askew,
The music of laughter flows freely, it's true.

Tickling the ivories of whimsical dreams,
Each note a delight, bursting at the seams.
The laughter in lyrics, soft whispers of fun,
In this concert of giggles, there's room for each pun.

So gather your friends for this heart-lighting show,
In the symphony's grace, let the laughter all flow.
For the harmonies clashing are songs of the heart,
A raucous rendition, a comical art.

With each trill and giggle, we'll dance through the night,
In the buoyant embrace of joy, love takes flight.
In this grand orchestra, with laughter we start,
Finding the rhythm in harmonies of heart.

Nature's Stanza of Color

In a garden where colors play,
Sunflowers giggle in bright array,
Daisies dance in a silly spin,
While butterflies tease with a cheeky grin.

Roses wear hats of dewy mist,
Tulips take part in a prank-filled twist,
A breezy breeze with a whimsical hum,
Makes cricket jokes that leave us numb.

Laughter echoes from lily pads,
As frogs in tuxedos jump in their lads,
Petunias snicker in shades of hue,
While bees take bets on the nectar brew.

All around, nature's merry jest,
Where colors frolic, they're at their best,
A vibrant party, wild and spry,
With petals chatting as clouds drift by.

The Palette of the Wordsmith

With a brush dipped in laughter's hue,
The wordsmith paints tales that feel brand new,
Each verse a splash of vibrant charm,
Where humor tickles and won't disarm.

A limerick flows like a bubbling brook,
Every pun tucked like a sly little nook,
Colors of wit in quirky strands,
Tangled tales that dance like bands.

In the garden of phrases, joy does bloom,
A field of chuckles dispersing gloom,
Each syllable sprinkles like confetti bright,
A riot of letters to ignite delight.

From magical metaphors to playful rhymes,
Nature's own script in whimsical times,
In this lively palette, joy takes flight,
Crafting laughter in every line so light.

A Symphony of Flora

In the orchestra where daisies sing,
Guitar strumming comes from a bumblebee's wing,
The violets play the tambourine,
While the roses waltz, all dressed in green.

Each lilac note is a giggling sound,
As the ferns sway gently all around,
Sunflowers lead in a towering show,
With petals clapping, a cheerful blow.

A cactus hums a prickly tune,
While daisies giggle under the moon,
Nature's concert is a riot of cheer,
Where every bloom has a song to hear.

Harmony blooms in this playful space,
A symphony wrapped in nature's embrace,
And in this garden where laughter floats,
Even the mushrooms don little coats.

Tales from the Floral Haven

In a haven where flowers spin tales,
The tulips gossip like curious gales,
With roots that dig for the silliest news,
And daisies prank with colorful views.

The lilies chat over tea steeped in mirth,
While petunias toss quips about their birth,
Each bloom has wisdom, down to their cores,
Reading petals' secrets, like open doors.

A rose sneezes, and petals fall down,
While pansies giggle, wearing a crown,
In these narratives, life takes a turn,
And laughter ignites where flowers discern.

With every breeze, stories are spun,
In a world where humor and flora run,
The floral haven, so vivid and bright,
Weaves tales of jest in the soft twilight.

Blossoms in the Poet's Heart

In a garden of jokes, I like to roam,
Where tulips and puns call me home,
The daisies giggle, the roses prance,
While daffodils dream of a silly dance.

The sunflowers nod with a knowing grin,
As I scribble verses, let the fun begin.
Bees buzz along to my witty tunes,
While butterflies laugh at the silliest moons.

Each petal a quip, each stem a jest,
Nature's own humor, at its very best.
With laughter like pollen, it fills the air,
In this playful world, I have not a care.

So join in the fun, let's frolic and jest,
In this garden of mirth, where humor is blessed.
For laughter is magic, a flower that grows,
In the heart of the poet, where joy overflows.

Verses Beneath the Canopy

Under the trees, where the shadows play,
The squirrels are plotting some mischief today.
With acorns as ammo, they take their aim,
While I jot down lines and forget my shame.

Leaves whisper secrets, each rustle a laugh,
As I try to sculpt a poetic giraffe.
But giraffes aren't easy in a tree's embrace,
So I sketch a tree frog in a silly race.

The wind lends its voice, oh what a thrill,
It tickles my thoughts, like a roller-coaster hill.
I write about giggles and whimsical sights,
Frogs dancing in slippers beneath starry nights.

So come to the canopy, let worries depart,
Where verses and laughter play a fine part.
In the shade of delight, the world seems so bright,
As we craft funny tales till the end of the night.

Florets of Imagination

With petals of nonsense and stems made of glee,
I planted a garden where fancies run free.
The wind carries whispers of quirky delight,
As I craft little stories to brighten the night.

The daisies plot plays, while the lilacs all cheer,
For the sunrise brings coffee and giggles to steer.
I sip on my laughter, it tickles the soul,
As I bounce ideas like spring's playful toll.

In a mix of colors, my thoughts intertwine,
With a sprinkle of humor, the stars realign.
The roses recite their best jokes from the past,
While the violets burst into fits that don't last.

So wander with me through this garden of fun,
Where each floret shares joy until day is done.
Let's share all the laughter that blooms in our mind,
For in the realm of dreams, there's no trouble to find.

Melodies from the Petal Path

On a pathway of petals, I hum and I sway,
With a chorus of critters who join in the play.
The crickets recite funny tales of their night,
While the ladybugs twirl in a dance of pure light.

Each flower a note, in this grand, joyful song,
Where the frogs croak the rhythm, all night long.
I skip over puddles, splashing with glee,
As the daisies all chant, 'Come dance with me!'

A whimsical breeze brings the smiles close at hand,
And the sun beams down like a spotlight so grand.
Together we giggle, as petals take flight,
Twirling and whirling in the soft moonlight.

So let's prance on this path where the magic won't cease,
With laughter that lingers, a moment of peace.
In the garden of music, we'll sing with delight,
For the joy of the petals keeps our hearts light.

Ink and Flora Entwined

In the garden, quills take flight,
With petals talking through the night.
The daisies jest, the roses rhyme,
As matter quickly turns to mime.

Words roll off, like springtime dew,
While tulips share their mad debut.
A sunflower tells a joke so bright,
The bumblebees just laugh in flight.

Ink spills colors, making friends,
With leafy lines that twist and bend.
A haiku sits upon the leaf,
And everyone's a poet, brief.

So in this patch where thoughts collide,
Blooming words run wild with pride.
Laughter echoes, fills the air,
Each line a petal, strange and rare.

Fragrance of Forgotten Lines

Old poems linger in the breeze,
Each stanza dressed in leafy teas.
The hyacinths hum tunes of yore,
While bromeliads sneak out for more.

A cactus claims it penned a sonnet,
While violets parade without a bonnet.
Dandelions puff up with pride,
Telling stories that they hide.

With every gust, old verses swirl,
Pollen dances, banners unfurl.
The lilac sneezes, off it goes,
King of laughter, as everybody knows.

So let the blooms of humor sprout,
In whimsical lines, let laughter shout.
Each forgotten word finds its place,
In the fragrant world, a funny embrace.

Nature's Poetic Canvas

Upon the earth, the verse is sown,
With roots that speak in tones well-known.
A canvas painted with delight,
As daisies giggle in the light.

The willow whispers witty tales,
While marigolds don fragrant veils.
Each brushstroke made of vine and leaf,
Spins nature's yarn, beyond belief.

Petunias scheme with jokes to share,
As butterflies flit without a care.
The earth's palette, full of jest,
In this wild jest, we are most blessed.

So let the blooms spread mirthful cheer,
In nature's art, there's laughter near.
Where petals sway and verses play,
A joyful heart is on display.

The Blooming Quatrain

Four lines in chorus, singers rise,
With lilies laughing, oh surprise!
Tulips titter at the pun,
Nature's giggle has begun.

The boughs and blooms join in the rhyme,
In perfect sync, they mock time.
With every breeze, a chuckle plays,
In this garden, we count the days.

Roses wink in red delight,
While marigolds join in the fight.
A droll quatrain spins around,
With laughter planted underground.

So here we gather, bright and bold,
In floral circles, tales unfold.
Each line a laugh, each petal cheer,
In blooming quatrains, joy is clear.

Rhythms Among the Flowers

In the garden, bees do dance,
With little hats, they take a chance.
They buzz all day, they sing their tune,
While flowers giggle, 'Who needs a boon?'

The tulips twirl, with swaying grace,
They wink at petals, a cheeky race.
Daisies laugh, they tell a joke,
While sunflowers grin, the best bespoke.

The roses gossip, oh what a sight,
About the weeds who lack their might.
"Why don't you bloom?" they tease with flair,
"We wear our colors, beyond compare!"

At dusk they gather, a petal band,
With leaf-shaped drums and a root contraband.
They sing of sun, they dance in glee,
In this floral ball, they're wild and free.

Petal Whispers of the Heart

A daffodil winks, all sunny and bright,
Saying, "Hey tulip, you dance just right!"
They shimmy and shake in the warm spring air,
While daisies gossip, without a care.

The violets murmur sweet little tunes,
Under the watch of the chuckling moons.
"Oh dear rose, why do you pout?"
She replies, "Too many bees, I want to shout!"

The larkspur leaps, so tall and proud,
After facing storms, they've drawn a crowd.
"Join us, dear friends, let's make a scene,"
While petals giggle, they're all so keen.

With every breeze, they share a sigh,
Oh how they twist, oh how they fly.
These cheeky blooms, filled with mirth,
In this silly patch, they reign the earth.

Secrets of the Swaying Branches

In the orchard, secrets thrive,
Where apples whisper, and pears arrive.
The branches sway, with a giggle so light,
As squirrels play pranks from morn till night.

Beneath the boughs, a rabbit hops,
With tiny sneakers, he never stops.
"Catch me if you can!" he calls with glee,
While overhead, the birds watch free.

The cherries chuckle, they know the game,
As the fruit flies down, without any shame.
"We'll have a feast, come join our fun!"
They lure in friends with laughter spun.

The wind joins in, with a playful peek,
Making leaves dance, in a cheeky streak.
So here in the grove, joy takes a chance,
Among swinging branches, all join the dance.

The Hymn of the Blooms

Upon the breeze, a melody flows,
From lilies that sway and a dahlia that glows.
They sing out loud with a harmony bright,
"Life is a garden, let's dance in the light!"

The peonies twirl, in dresses so grand,
While zinnias boast of their colorful band.
Every flower knows, they're meant to play,
In this quirky opera, come what may.

The violets chuckle, "We're tiny and cute,
But we'll steal the show in our best little suit!"
With petals aglow, they take their stage,
Each giggling flower writes a new page.

So let the blooms raise their voices high,
With laughter and joy that fills the sky.
For in this garden, where chaos abounds,
A silly hymn of cheer always surrounds.

Fables in a Flower Field

In a field where daisies laugh,
A bee forgot its own giraffe.
It buzzed around a tulip's hat,
While a caterpillar sang to a cat.

The sun wore sunglasses, oh so bright,
While shadows danced in pure delight.
A rabbit tried a sassy flip,
But landed in a buttercup dip.

The flowers chattered, sharing tales,
Of bees who thought they could grow scales.
A worm declared it's quite absurd,
For dirt's the only suit it's heard.

And so the fables weave and flow,
Where silly stories regularly grow.
A giggle here, a chuckle there,
In a field where laughter fills the air.

The Serenity of Swaying Blooms

In the breeze, they do a jig,
Watching daisies chugging a big swig.
A sunflower twirled like a clumsy star,
With roots that wandered oh so far.

The lilacs giggle in the sun,
Whispering secrets, it's all in fun.
A tulip with a monocle so grand,
Sipped on tea from a dainty hand.

Bumblebees join in with a dance,
While butterflies spin, lost in a trance.
A ladybug rolls over with glee,
Saying, "Life's just a wild jubilee!"

As colors sway and laughter beams,
The meadow hosts the silliest dreams.
With petals bright, they laugh and spin,
In this joyous world, where all begin.

Hues of Heartfelt Lyrics

Petunias wrote a love ballad,
With notes that twisted and swayed so salad.
A chorus of violets chimed in tune,
While daisies tapped their toes by the moon.

The roses blushed, oh what a sight,
With love letters tied to every light.
A flower pot pondered jokes so clever,
As sunbeams fell like fiery feathers.

Ferns whispered puns, both silly and sweet,
While zinnias decorated with dance on their feet.
A cacti swayed to a prickly beat,
In this garden, where hearts skip sweet.

The ink of petals painted with cheer,
As laughter rang in blooms so near.
With every hue telling its tale,
A song of joy wafts in the gale.

The Dancers of the Meadow

Under skies of blue with cotton candy fluff,
Petals twirl as if to say, "That's enough!"
A pollen party starts at noon,
While grasshoppers play a rhythmical tune.

Daffodils stretch, oh what a pose,
While busy daisies wear frilly clothes.
A dandelion cheered, with seeds galore,
Shouting, "Let's dance, who could ask for more?"

With blooms in costumes, quite the array,
Each flower shines in its own way.
A funky fern grooves side to side,
With all of nature as its guide.

So come to the meadow, leave worries behind,
Join in this dance, where joy's redefined.
For laughter and cheer spill from each flower,
The meadow's alive with blissful power.

The Song of Swaying Lilies

In the garden a lily sways,
Tickling the wind in silly ways.
It dances and twirls in sheer delight,
Daring the bees to join the flight.

A frog hops by, gives a sigh,
"What's with the moves? Are you shy?"
The lily just laughs and replies,
"I'm practicing for the big dance prize!"

A breeze whispers tunes, oh so sweet,
As the lily grooves to its own heartbeat.
Join in the fun, come take a chance,
Who knew the flowers could really dance?

The sun rolls in, it's time to shine,
Lilies sway along the vine.
With leaves as fans, they steal the show,
Nature's cabaret, don't you know?

Sunlight on Delicate Leaves

Sunlight giggles on gentle leaves,
Painting patterns, like playful thieves.
Each glimmer a wink, a cheeky tease,
While squirrels plot pranks with utmost ease.

A leaf blushes bright, catches the sun,
"You think I'm cute? Well, that's just fun!"
Along comes a breeze, joins in the cheer,
"Don't leaf me hanging, come dance, my dear!"

Together they sparkle under blue skies,
With shadows and laughter, a funny guise.
The sunshine grins, throws its rays,
As leaves giggle in hazy ballet.

A robin joins in, with chirps so spry,
"I'm here for the show! What's life without sky?"
And all the leaves sway like they're in a band,
Under the sun, nature's stage is grand!

Motifs in the Meadow

In a meadow bright, where daisies play,
A fox trots by, but hey —no way!
"Did you see that?" the flowers giggle,
As the fox trips up, doing a little wiggle.

Butterflies flutter, their colors so bold,
Whispering secrets, tales yet untold.
"Let's paint the air!" the daisies exclaim,
"A canvas of joy, let's play this game!"

A rabbit appears, with ears in the air,
"Is that a dance? Or just a hair scare?"
"It's the motif of fun, can't you see?"
With giggles and leaps, they all agree.

In this lovely glade, laughter does bloom,
With each silly step, it fills the room.
As the sun dips low, the fun won't cease,
In the meadow of mirth, they find their peace.

The Unwritten Blossom

In a garden of thoughts, where laughter grows,
An unwritten flower, nobody knows.
It peeks out shyly, with dreams in its head,
Saying, "I'm not sure if I want to spread!"

With petals of ideas and stamen of might,
"Shall I bloom now, or wait for the night?"
A bee buzzes by, with a knowing grin,
"Oh come on, dear friend, let the fun begin!"

The flower chuckles, gives in to the brunt,
"Alright, let's see if I can pull off a stunt!"
It opens up wide with a glorious flair,
And the whole garden can't help but stare.

"What's next?" it asks, all eager and spry,
"Shall we dance with the wind, wave to the sky?"
Now that it's written, the blossom prances free,
Turning the ordinary into comedy!

Vignettes in Vibrant Greens

In a garden full of cheer,
Plants whisper tales you'll hear.
A dandelion wears a crown,
While the violets dance around.

A lazy bee buzzes high,
Forgetting how to say goodbye.
With pollen stuck to its knees,
It's wondering, "Where's the next breeze?"

The snails plot a race so slow,
Betting on who'll steal the show.
While worms giggle in a heap,
Dreaming of a soil-bound leap.

Lettuce tries to play a tune,
Underneath the laughing moon.
Each carrot sings with leafy glee,
As radishes roll in jubilee.

The Voice of the Verdant

The trees wear hats made of moss,
Feeling fashion's lovely gloss.
While squirrels debate the latest trends,
Pinecones watch as laughter bends.

The ivy tickles the old brick wall,
Mossy laughter begins to sprawl.
A hedgehog juggles acorns with flair,
And no one knows how he got there.

The daisies gossip 'bout the sun,
Who clearly thinks he's so much fun.
As shadows stretch across the grass,
The daisies plot a game to pass.

A frog leaps high with a goofy grin,
Practicing for his hop-along win.
With every jump, he croaks a joke,
While lily pads start to gently croak.

Echoes from Petal Fields

In a field where laughter grows,
The tulips tell the silliest prose.
Each petal twirls like it's on a spree,
While daisies giggle in harmony.

Sunflowers stretch for a cheeky peek,
Their secret's out—they love to sneak.
They whisper to the passing breeze,
"Just wait till we tango with the bees!"

A butterfly flaunts its fanciest attire,
While caterpillars aspire to retire.
With each wobble, they trip and fall,
Turning dancing into a crawl.

The grasshoppers play a banjo tune,
While crickets dance beneath the moon.
They laugh at clouds that start to roll,
For giggles give the heart console.

Strokes of Nature's Brush

A painter squirrel with a little brush,
Creates a masterpiece in a rush.
With splashes of acorn and berry hues,
He giggles as his art renews.

The pond reflects a wacky crew,
A fish with glasses waving, "Hello, too!"
Egrets in tuxedos make a scene,
While frogs applaud their leafy green.

A ladybug struts — she's dressed to kill,
With polka dots that give a thrill.
She twirls and spins among the moss,
While beetles cheer, "You're the boss!"

In this canvas where laughter reigns,
Nature's joy spills through the veins.
With every chuckle, colors blend,
In a world where fun will never end.

The Flourishing Stanza

In the garden of rhyme they sprout,
Words dance about with laughter and shout.
A daisy tells jokes to a tulip so grand,
While a rogue little weed takes a stand.

Petals swap stories in bright sunny light,
They chuckle and giggle from morning till night.
Every stanza's a party, a merry old scene,
With verses like confetti, all sprightly and keen.

The bees hum the tunes of a pun-laden song,
While butterflies flutter, joining in along.
Each line is a joke, each stanza a spree,
In this floral fiesta, come join with me!

So here's to the blooms, both silly and wise,
Planting laughter in ink, let your wit rise.
A garden of gags, where we frolic and play,
In the flourishing stanza, all worries go away.

Serendipity in Full Bloom

One sunny morning, a bloom took a chance,
Wiggled its petals, eager to dance.
A bumblebee giggled, pollen in tow,
Spinning in circles, putting on a show.

The daisies debated, who could be best,
One claimed a crown, the other, a jest.
With laughter contagious, they spun through the air,
Planting joy everywhere, without a care.

A rose tried to rhyme with the lavender's hue,
But stumbled on syllables, oh what a view!
The mischief of petals drew laughter from all,
As they tumbled and twirled in a floral free-for-all.

So when life seems rooted, just take a good look,
There's humor in nature, if you read the book.
With petals around you, you'll soon find the tune,
In serendipity's bloom, let hilarity croon.

The Poet's Floral Reverie

In a patch of bright colors, the poet awoke,
Finding wisdom in petals, and joy in each poke.
A sunflower winked, while the violets snickered,
As the gallant old daffodil boldly flickered.

The thorns gathered round for a gossip-filled chat,
They whispered of tulips and debated the brat.
Petals were flapping, oh, what a delight,
When a gust of hot wind sent them into flight!

A lilac laughed loud, mixed prose with a pun,
While the fragrant old rose said, "Oh, let's have fun!"
Each verse had its quirk, each word wore a smile,
In this whimsical garden, joy stretched for a mile.

So raise up your verses, let laughter take flight,
In the poet's sweet reverie, everything's bright.
With flowers and humor, life's a grand spree,
Where every petal whispers, "Come laugh here with me!"

An Ode to the Wild Petals

Oh, wild little petals, how jolly you sway,
With antics and giggles, you brighten the day.
A poppy once joked with a ragged old thorn,
"Your fashion's a gamble, I'd hang out at dawn!"

Each flower a character, quirky and spry,
As bees took the stage, buzzing by and by.
A daffodil chuckled, "I'm all about cheer,
And my friend the bluebell draws crowds when he's here!"

The wind brought a tune, oh, what a grand tune,
As petals all twirled, like a merry cartoon.
"Let's dance till it's dusk," cried a brave little bud,
While giggling together, they embraced the mud.

To wild petals we raise a toast, oh so true,
With laughter and color, the world feels anew.
In a garden of comedy, let our joys unfold,
An ode to the wild, where the funny is gold.

www.ingramcontent.com/pod-product-compliance
Lightning Source LLC
Chambersburg PA
CBHW071831160426
43209CB00003B/275